Path *of* Life
Reflections of a Soul in Bloom

Tirzah Nilsson

DiViNE PURPOSE
publishing house
Fort Worth, TX

Path of Life: Reflections of a Soul in Bloom
© 2025 Tirzah Nilsson

Scripture quotations are from the ESV® Bible (The Holy Bible, English Standard Version®), © 2001 by Crossway, a publishing ministry of Good News Publishers. ESV Text Edition: 2025. The ESV text may not be quoted in any publication made available to the public by a Creative Commons license. The ESV may not be translated in whole or in part into any other language. Used by permission. All rights reserved.

No part of this book may be reproduced in any form, stored in a retrieval system, or transmitted in any form by any means—electronic, mechanical, photocopy, recording, or any other—except for brief quotations in printed reviews, without the prior written permission of the copyright owner.

DiViNE Purpose Publishing House LLC
Fort Worth, TX 76131
www.divinepurposepublishing.com

Library of Congress Control Number: 2025911135

ISBN 978-1-948812-40-5

For Emma, the bosom friend who read and even helped write all my poems for so many years and whose life intertwined with mine to bring many of the trials and joys that helped me grow into who I am today.

Contents

I. Cute, Funny, Whimsical

If I Were You and You Were Me	15
My Day	17
Time	18
Independence Day	19
A Little White Cat	22
My Kitty Cat	23
Devil's Horse	24
The Glass Window	26
Yesterday Night At Six O' Clock	27
My Kitten	29
Bedtime Thoughts	30
Dream of the Stars	32
Dreamland	33
Her Touch Is Death: A Duck's Tale	34

II. Beauty & Appreciation

My Joy	39
God's Sunrise	40
Burnished Gold	41
They Tell of Their Creator	43
Eagle of Our Nation	45
Liberty Stallion	46
Rainbow of Flowers	52
The Snow Queen	54
A Welcome Storm	56

A Raindrop's Tale	57
Dream Garden	59
Gypsy Music	60
Springtime Song	62
The Racetrack Rainbow	63
My Garden	64
Autumn Beauty	65
Prisoners of White	66
Oh, the Beauty of Winter!	68
The West is on Fire!	70
God's Evening Cure	71
Evening Peace	72
A Cold, Clear Night	73
The Pretty Blue Moon	74

III. Life, Faith, Relationship

Half Past Thirteen	79
What Do You See?	80
My Love For You	83
Flash Flood in My Heart	84
My Calling	86
In the Shadow of His Hand	88
Psalm 23	89
Help Me	91
The Only Good Thing	92
Little By Little	94
I Trust You	97
My Story	100
Path of Life	103
Love of My Life	107

My Hands	109
The Cry of My Heart	110
It Could Have Been	113
Dreams and Fantasy	115
Poison in My Mind	116
What is Emotion?	117
Someday Perhaps	118
Mark Upon My Heart	120
Can I Trust Again?	122
This Shallow Life	124
Something Missing	126
The Hidden Truth	128
I Want the Real You Back	131
Fight or Acquiesce	132
It Matters Not What Others Think	135
"I Will Not Compromise"	136
Appreciation	138
A Lesson From the Shadows	139
Little Miss Sunshine	141
Where Beauty Lies	143
A Song of Good News	144
The Story for the Story	148
Confetti Sprinkles	150
Happy New Year	151

About the Author

Dear Reader,

Hi! My name is Tirzah. I'm really excited to share some of my poetry with you! First, I'd love to talk a little bit about myself and my story as I invite you to see the world through my eyes in the poems I've written over the years.

I've been passionately in love with words and intrigued by the different ways they can be used for as long as I can remember, and my English education has primarily come just from reading a wide variety of books from many different time periods during my early years. My earliest clear memory of attempting to write my own story was when I was seven, and I started playing with rhythm and rhyme when I was nine or ten. Immediately fascinated, I began writing my own poetry quite regularly. The earliest poems included in this collection were written when I was ten or eleven, and while a few are more recent, the majority come from the time period when I was between thirteen and fifteen.

For the sake of context, I was thirteen and a half when the pandemic started and had a lot of free time at that point. Later in 2020 is when my life really got crazy though, when my best friend's mental health started spiraling and this spilled over onto me and began to wreck mine too. As someone who was homeschooled my entire life and didn't have access to the internet, I also started to see the world for what it was around this time, through my church and my friend sharing her struggles at school. Confused and broken, I didn't know what to do with myself. Everything I had known and believed was being challenged. I wasn't sure if I should dive into the crazy normal teen world and engage in popular behaviors and sources of entertainment that didn't seem appropriate to me, or refrain and stay isolated and alone. In my desperation, I turned to the word of God and was soon convinced that, *like it or not*, He did not condone the things of the world, and the right path could only be to stay strong and *not* become one with the world.

I wrote a lot about my feelings, the reasons for my choices, relationships with people and God, and my desperation to help others see the truth that He alone can save them, and that He holds the answers to all of our problems. The wild thing is, I was actually a brand-new believer at the time. Raised in church my entire life, I did not develop a relationship with the Lord for myself before 2020. It truly blows my mind the way He moved to stir me to come closer to Him *just before* everything went crazy – my titular poem *Path of Life* (page 103) refers to this as it mentions how I had no idea what I was missing until He gently woke me to His love and the state of my life. From my perspective, it was me giving Him a chance to show me why it mattered how I lived my life and what being a Christian meant, but now I know that He knew I needed Him then and both nudged me to ask my questions and met me there to make it real when I started reading His Word.

Looking back, when I read my work from those years, I'm amazed. I tend to forget, over and over, these lessons I clearly learned at that time, and need the reminders again. It blows my mind to see the simple wisdom I managed to derive from God's word at such a young age, and I can't help but wonder at the childlike faith so clearly demonstrated in almost every piece.

When God told me to publish a collection of poetry, I wondered for a minute whether it should include just the poems about my life journey, or also the ones about cute kittens, silly ideas, and funny stories with no real moral value, but it was not hard to see that presenting the full picture of my early years was best accomplished by sharing a wide variety of everything that interested me! Besides, many of these cute, whimsical poems are simply delightful and may bring a rare sort of smile to the reader's face, just by their innocence and beauty. My prayer is that the mixture of lighthearted joy with my childlike approach to the deep problems we all encounter over and over in our lives will gladden your heart while also reminding you of the simple truths of God's word – things that we as adults so often try to complicate far beyond what they were meant to be.

Oddly enough, because of the way I was raised and where my literary influences came from, I don't write like anyone else in my generation – probably not like anyone else at all, actually – so somehow, what I've been told is that my poetry tends to be relatable to readers of all ages. Certainly, it is my hope that everyone who reads this collection will come away with something uniquely encouraging and that it will brighten your eyes and strengthen your heart as you read it.

I.
Cute, Funny, Whimsical

Cute, Funny, Whimsical

If I Were You and You Were Me

If I were you and you were me,
How very different that would be!
You'd live in my house, I in yours,
And I would have to do your chores.

If you were me and I were you,
Who could tell, then, who'd be who?
I know I'm *me*, and *you're* <u>yourself</u> –
And I can't *help* but be *my*self!

If I were you and you were me,
I think that I'd so addled be,
I wouldn't know blue sky from bricks,
And could I even count to six?

If you were me and I were you,
Would four be made of six plus two?
Perhaps cold ice would burn your mouth…
Maybe the sun would set in the south?

If I were you and you were me,
We might find coffee in our tea.
Or Mars might suddenly turn green
Or maybe purple in between.

If you were me and I were you,
Pink might be brown, or yellow blue.
The sun, it might just disappear,
And for all I know, we'd still be here.

Path of Life

You know, I think I'll not complain,
Though we miss out on Ice Cream Rain;
If you stay you and I stay I,
I will not make a single cry.

My Day

When the morning sun is rising
And pink is in the east,
I am happy and excited
'Bout the new day come to feast.

When the noontime sun is high,
I'm the busiest of all.
I don't have time to rest,
Or think about a ball.

When the evening sun is sinking
And there's orange in the west
I am glad the day is over!
I'm ready for my rest!

When, at midnight, in the sky,
The moon is shining down,
I'm safe in bed, my head on pillow,
Sleeping very sound.

Time

The hours and minutes go slow,
But the days go fast.
Tomorrow will never come,
But now it's past.

The days go by faster,
The minutes yet slow,
As, year by year,
Much older I grow.

This thing called Time,
How does it work?
When I try to stop it,
It goes berserk.

It goes quickly for me;
Not for children, you know,
And still I remember
It seeming so slow.

And so, I am sure
For those older than me,
It goes quicker still,
And will keep speeding, see?

Time is confusing,
Time is unreal.
I wish time were different –
So dizzy I feel!

Independence Day

"Independence Day is coming!"
The kids cry out in glee,
"The time for glow sticks, fireworks,
And red, white, blue candy!

"We'll get to play with sparklers
And stay up late at night!
And while we watch excitedly,
They'll color the dark sky bright!

"There'll be cookies, oh, and cake,
And lots of candy too.
There'll be parades and banners
Colored red and white and blue!"

"I see," said Grandpa, "that you well
Know *how* to celebrate.
But, I wonder, do you know
Just *why* this day is great?"

They thought, then said, "Why, no, we don't,
It really isn't clear.
The *reason* that we celebrate?
Please tell us, Grandpa dear."

So he smiled, sat them down,
Then said, importantly,
"Why, kids, this day's the greatest
In our country's history!

Path of Life

"This day, in seventeen seventy-six,
Brave men named the day
To celebrate an act they did
Two days before, I say.

"July the second, they signed a page
That Thomas Jefferson wrote.
It said they held themselves as free
From the so-called lobster-coats.

"And fight they did – oh, what a fight!
'Til at last King George agreed.
But it started on July the fourth,
A great day in history!

"So the reason that we celebrate
Is not just for our fun.
It's to celebrate our country's birth,
Year two hundred fifty-one!

"It's to recall that freedom spirit
True Americans all possess!
So listen, kids, and don't forget,
Our country needs your best!

"So give your all to keep men free,
Our country still untamed.
Don't let them take it from you, kids;
It's mine and yours, the same!"

Cute, Funny, Whimsical

The kids, with awestruck voices, say,
"We get it, Grandpa, yes!
We'll tell our friends, and all of us
Will always do our best!

"We *will* preserve our country's life;
Its light will never dim!
Not if *we* can help it, sir.
We'll do our best for kin!"

A Little White Cat

A little white cat has stolen my heart
By tripping on airy feet
Into the place where I keep my heart;
I love my kitten so sweet!

A little white cat has demanded my love
By tripping on soft white paws
Into the place where is made my love;
I love her, not knowing the cause!

A little white cat said "love only me"
By making a pretty purr
Which reaches clear to the middle of me;
Of cats, I love only her!

My Kitty Cat

It took me by surprise,
This little kitty cat.
Its pretty, pale blue eyes,
The queenly way it sat.

Her pretty, soft white fur,
Her gorgeous, light blonde tail;
The way she watched my lure,
Assured that it would fail.

Her excited kitten's eyes,
Her snowy, soft white paws,
That capture passing flies
To eat without a cause.

My darling sweet cute cat,
What pictures you do make
As you play with my old hat!
My own sweet white Snowflake.

Devil's Horse

There's a horse that must be the devil's own;
He jumps and bucks in a class alone.
No man could ride this bronc, I'm sure.
I tried and landed in the dirt.

Up with his heels, and away we go:
Up and down, and around – oh no!
He kicks again and I land with a thud,
Upside down in a pile of mud.

Well, I didn't get up too fast.
In fact, I thought I'd breathed my last.
I hurt all over, yes, real bad.
They say he'd only worked a tad!

The news spread quickly, far and wide.
Folks came and they tried to ride.
It didn't go too well, I say!
No one ever got to stay.

Then, one day, there came a girl,
Young and pretty, her hair in a curl.
She went and opened up his gate,
And folks were sure they knew her fate.

But she went up to him and said,
To that hunk of horse with the devil's head,
"Why, you darling sweet thing, you,
I know you've good inside, you do."

Cute, Funny, Whimsical

Folks, they gasped, and yelled at her,
"Hey, you best get out of there!
He'll paw you to a pulp, he will!
Get out, why are you standing still?"

But he nuzzled at her hair,
And seemed to want to keep her there.
She offered him a treat. He thought,
Then took it with a friendly nod.

Then she did what none had done:
She patted his glossy coat of dun!
After a minute she called for a stool,
Then climbed upon his back, the fool!

But, this stallion – surely no!
He took her where she wished to go.
She put her arms around his neck
And whispered in his ear a sec.

You wouldn't believe it! I hardly did –
This devil's horse loving that pretty kid.
But that girl, I tell you, she rode away,
On the devil's horse, only yesterday!

The Glass Window

The cat who sat upon the sill
Crouched to watch, perfectly still.
No muscle moved in all his might;
Only his tail and eyes alight.

So rigid, so careless of all behind,
His mind and his senses trained outside;
He sat so poised for many a minute
Before at the last giving up on it.

Turning around, he asks for a pet.
It's easy to see the disappointment.
Oh, how he wonders what's out there,
Out of the house in the fresh, clean air.

Happy he is, but he wishes to be
Out where the world is real and green.
Out where living things move and grow,
Just outside of the glass window.

Cute, Funny, Whimsical

Yesterday Night At Six O' Clock

Yesterday night, when I saw the moon,
'Twas big and orange, quite like a balloon.
Twelve hours before you'd hear the crow's cock,
Yesterday night at six o' clock.

We were driving on the road in a small white car
Too early to see, in the heavens, a star,
When the pretty moon heralded nightfall's tock,
Yesterday night at six o' clock.

In the sky, you saw the sun's goodnight:
"Goodnight," said he, "enjoy the moonlight!"
Though pink and gold the moon did mock,
Yesterday night at six o' clock.

Coming over the dark green trees,
Enjoying the very cold winter breeze,
He came, the beauty of night to unlock,
Yesterday night at six o' clock.

Dressed in a gold and orange robe,
He paid us a visit from over the globe.
He came as a prince, no cheap-made smock
Wore he last night at six o' clock.

After a while he faded away,
To become the moon of every day.
After telling you, "wear your socks"
Yesterday night at six o' clock.

Path of Life

On the horizon, near no city,
It was so very, very pretty;
You'd 'most not rather drive than walk,
Yesterday night at six o' clock.

Cute, Funny, Whimsical

My Kitten

I have a kitten who's very cute;
He sits in the palm of my hand.
He's white with gray on his ears and tail,
And he lives off the fat of the land.

His name is Blizzard; he's my very own
And has been since he was born.
His eyes are blue, his hair is long,
And all lesser cats he scorns.

Path of Life

Bedtime Thoughts

When I go to bed tonight,
Before I fall asleep,
I'll think of anything except
The morning's dreaded beep.

I'll worry not about the time,
Nor tomorrow's work.
I'll think not of my tiredness;
No, such thoughts I shirk!

Instead I'll think about my day,
Of all that I did wrong;
I also think of things that make
Me feel my life's a song!

What some person did or said
That made my heart feel glad;
What I did to shame myself
(For I was really bad!)

Or I think of future days
(This path more oft I choose)…
I dream that all my dreams come true;
Of sleeping, what's the use?

While yet awake, I dream so real,
Of romance, friends, fame, tragedy.
I dream I'm brave, and strong, and smart –
The hero every time, you see.

Cute, Funny, Whimsical

But, alas, it all must end,
I must come back to truth.
And go to sleep, so that I can
In fact, maintain my youth.

Dream of the Stars

Before you go to sleep tonight,
Look out at the evening light
Shining from the moon.
Many a star is in the sky,
Telling you "goodnight, goodbye,
We'll see you very soon."

For when you close your eyes you may
Take a trip through the Milky Way –
Maybe even touch a star!
Sailing through the heavens with ease,
Going whichever way you please,
To a place so very far.

Dreamland

When you close your weary eyes,
You are in for a surprise.
When you open them again,
Life will not be good as then.

For when you close your eyes, oh my!
Peppermint hills and berry sky,
Minty trees and sugar sand,
Many a bonbon in your hand.

Chocolate dogs and candy cats.
The cattle's poops are sugar splats!
A cookie horse takes you to your
House of candy canes galore.

You nibble sugar from its mane
And watch it leave on Maple Lane –
But wait! A gumdrop doorknob you invites
To taste its very yummy bites.

You turn the knob and step inside
In time to see a candy slide
And worlds of sticky apple juice…
Why, here's a Snickers on the loose!

But, alas! Your 'larm clock rings,
Calling you to boring things;
For you must many things complete
Before again you dream of sweet.

Her Touch Is Death: A Duck's Tale

Early this morning, at eight o' clock,
My friends and I stood 'round,
Hissing conspiratorially
And dirtying up the ground.

When one of the people, a tall one,
Came toward us, and we knew
That on this day her touch was death –
Her eye contained the clue!

For we've all learned this certain look
They give us just this way;
It means they plan to roast us;
Her touch is death today!

So we turned and waddled away,
As fast as ever we could.
Hurry, hurry! We know for sure
Her touch is death's black hood.

She's far too close; quick, scatter, now!
It's every duck on his own!
Oh no, still she's following *me!*
Her touch is death, 'tis known!

She's closing in; I must evade
The corner – now I'm free!
But alas, she's still on my heels.
Her touch is death to me.

Cute, Funny, Whimsical

Now she's started moving faster!
I try to faster go…
But with a leap, she's got me.
I'm marked for death, I know.

She locked me up inside a cage.
I checked the door; it's tight.
Now I see them setting up
To end me later tonight.

My life's as good as over;
I'll never get away.
But, fellow-ducks, remember:
Her touch is death, I say!

II.

Beauty & Appreciation

My Joy

It's such a lovely day today,
Though I could not say why.
I feel a great excitement,
But don't know why so high.

I just woke up this morning,
And when I got out of bed
I found my thoughts so happy
I could dance, and on my head!

My God is good, my God is great;
He gives me all I need!
My joy is found in Him today
As from old chains I'm freed!

Path of Life

God's Sunrise

As the sun rises,
I take a deep breath
Filled with the truth
Of this lovely life's wealth.

I cannot express
The excitement I feel!
It is so amazing
I cannot hold still.

I must dance, sing, and shout
My praise to the King
Who made all this bliss
Just to make my nerves ring.

I can't hold it in;
I laugh loud and long!
I cannot stop singing
My wonderful song.

Burnished Gold

In a wide and sunlit meadow,
Grazing, full of peace,
Are many geldings, mares, and colts,
Of pretty colors, these.

But in the center one of them,
Quite unafraid and bold,
Paws the ground and draws eyes to
His coat of burnished gold.

In this group that's full of bays,
With many a shade of dun,
It's clear that God made one of them
To shine just like the sun.

His mane and tail of silver shine,
A color looking cold,
To offset the warmth in the rest of his
Great coat of burnished gold.

His haunches gleam, his muscles show;
He seems to start a dance.
His beauty and his power both
Displayed in the mighty prance.

He turned around, he's coming back,
And as he comes, behold!
No other horse is quite like him;
His name is Burnished Gold!

Path of Life

As he rears and paws the air,
I know 'tis not a whim:
If you search all the world there's not
Another horse like him!

His head and tail he holds up high,
The perfect horse to mold.
The *least* amazing part of him,
His coat of burnished gold.

They Tell of Their Creator

One morning when I went outside
I looked around, then did decide
"I'll take a walk in the woods so green
And find what beauty is to be seen."

So off I went that warm spring day
And looked around along the way,
To find a clearing, wide and green,
Full of beauty to be seen.

Lots of lovely scents to smell;
Birdies singing, much to tell.
They tell of their Creator's goodness,
And His love for each new nest.

The flowers blooming, blue and gold,
Purple, pink, colors soft or bold!
They tell of their Creator's art,
Created but to gladden my heart.

The grass, beneath my feet, so soft,
The tumbling rabbits, playing oft –
They tell of their Creator's plan,
They tell it all throughout the land.

The butterflies flitting through the air,
The pond whose water ripples there,
They tell of their Creator who
Loves them, but, much more, me and you.

Path of Life

The wind, while whispering through the trees,
A couple of busy honeybees,
They tell of their Creator who
Died and rose for me and you.

Eagle of Our Nation

An eagle is a picture of our country,
An image of America the Free.
A look of fiercest freedom in his eye,
Untamable forever does he fly.

An eagle is the symbol of our nation,
And one which should provide us inspiration.
His broad wings always carry him above
The troubles borne by gentle-hearted doves.

The eagle is the spirit of our men;
The one which will yet make us great again.
He'll never yield; he'll die before he'll cave!
His courage rivals tales of all the brave.

Our eagle is the one to make us sure
We always must continue and endure;
Survive the darkest nights, the fiercest chill,
To save our freedom to do as we will.

Liberty Stallion

Like a horse who's galloping, wild and free,
That's how this country seems to be.
He's strong and fast and fierce and brave,
Yet kind and just and keeps no slave.

Back in seventeen seventy-three,
A young horse colt kicked to be free.
A docile horse was he back then,
Until he chose to break his pen.

Men together did unite,
Freedom in his eyes to light.
Now this eye contains a spark
Of freedom, all ye nations hark!

This horse his freedom soon will gain,
And then you all will feel the pain.
If then you try for something bad,
Beware lest you should make him mad!

Toward Lexington the British came,
And Paul Revere declared the same.
He rode that night in seventy-five,
So Minutemen could save their lives.

July the second, seventy-six,
We tired of King George's tricks.
The Declaration did we write,
Beginning now, for real, the fight.

Congress met and quickly chose
George Washington to fight the foes.
George's cold and hungry men
Fought the redcoats one to ten.

Our horse was almost beaten, but
His eyes were not completely shut.
He almost died at Valley Forge,
But rose again to fight with George.

Washington now has a hope;
Perhaps this colt can learn to lope.
On Yorktown he decides to march
Though men and dirt the sun will parch.

We won and now is gone the colt
That from a fight was wont to bolt.
A great big stallion's in his place,
And none can slow his steady pace.

With head and tail held high he stands;
Why should we meet their demands?
His head he tosses; stomps his foot,
His freedom proudly gives a look!

This stallion, symbol of liberty,
Is white to show his purity.
He wears red 'cause he's brave, and blue
Because he always says what's true.

Path of Life

He throws his head and proudly snorts,
While England's men are out of sorts.
His stance is full of manly pride,
While o'er the ground he seems to glide.

As he's galloping down the road,
He thinks he's changed from battle-mode…
But he was wrong; just thirty years
Since last this stallion beat his peers,

There comes another war so grim
A soldier's girl must cry for him.
The war of 1812 is here,
But our horse knows no human fear!

And so again, we win the war
Although our land's now battle-sore.
Again the victor, now we know
That over his neck no rope can go.

This stallion, symbol of liberty,
Snorts again, "I know I'm free,
For over my neck no rope can fly!
To enemies I say, 'goodbye!'"

So along came days of which you know,
Of cowboys and the Alamo.
Many died in Texas then,
To give their lives for other men.

Beauty & Appreciation

Many from other places came
To give their all for freedom's flame.
They fought that we might freedom keep,
That Texans might more calmly sleep.

This stallion was quite strong, you know.
All outward foes knew it was so!
Only one thing could take him out:
An inward parasitic sprout.

Then in April, eighteen sixty-one,
Brother fights brother; father, son!
The North and South will not agree –
Peace between them cannot be!

'Twas U.S. Grant, Abe Lincoln chose
To fight their rebellious southern bros;
The name they called his enemy
Was "General Robert Edward Lee."

You see what caused the Civil War:
From deep within, our country tore.
Each side thought that they knew best –
Which would pass the final test?

General Lee and his were poor
And lacked the funds for food and war,
Though lots of brains they had, it's true,
In General Jackson, and Jeb Stuart, too.

Path of Life

Some southern soldiers' accident
Set Lee to mourning in his tent;
He's lost, in Jackson, his best man,
And gave the North a greater chance.

For at this death the North grew strong,
Starting the end of the war so long.
'Twas admiration Lincoln won,
Besides the war, for it was done!

Instead of victory music he,
Our Lincoln, chose the song "Dixie;"
When, five days later, he was shot,
Many people prayed a lot.

The doctors watched him all night long;
The next day everything went wrong.
The fifteenth of April, sixty-five,
Our president ceased to be alive.

Our horse so strong began to quake;
Looked like disease his life would take.
With Lincoln's death his spirit quailed;
His steps slowed and began to fail.

Then, slowly at first, he began to revive,
And after a while, he started to thrive.
Our horse is past two hundred years;
It seems he's strong and has no fears.

But, whether you choose to believe it or not,
We do, in fact, have trouble a lot.
The parasites inside the horse,
If not destroyed, will cause remorse.

There's people who would rule the earth;
They're teaching lies about his birth.
They teach what's false to try to kill
This stallion who's the strongest still.

We must fight back! We must proclaim
The truth 'bout freedom's steady flame.
Reveal the truth, for much depends
On refusing what the world befriends.

Much has changed since our horse was born;
He's a stallion now, not a colt forlorn.
Though much has happened, still it's true,
One thing's unchanged for me and you:

The spirit of freedom we possess,
Which passes every single test.
We're always free, no man can tame
This horse whose spirit is freedom's flame.

Rainbow of Flowers

Out on the plains,
No humans are near.
I wish I could stay
Forever right here.

I sit in the sun
Wearing a smile,
Enjoying the breeze,
Not moving the while.

The soft green grass
Makes a rug for my feet;
The cool breezy wind
Brings a scent very sweet.

The smell of the flowers
In a meadow not far:
Bluebells and daisies,
And oh! A Texas Star!

I walk over there
For to see with my eyes,
And what I see makes me
Cry out with surprise!

All sorts of flowers
To tickle my nose!
Daffodils, tulips,
And a wild rose.

Dandelions, hyacinths,
Cornflowers blue.
Buttercups, poppies,
And snapdragons too.

Flowering bushes,
So many are here!
And all are quite pretty,
Of that have no fear!

Crepe myrtles, irises;
Some that, I say!
I neither know,
Nor have seen 'til today!

Oh what a rainbow
Of flowers galore!
There's many more too,
But I cannot say more.

Path of Life

The Snow Queen

The Snow Queen blossoms as a rose;
With white the pear tree overflows,
For springtime here has come again,
And small white flowers blossom then.

The beauty never lasts for long.
Just two weeks, maybe; then it's gone.
She's beautiful throughout the year,
But only Snow Queen truly, here.

She gathers all her petals white,
Then lets them kiss the stars at night.
And, for the summer, dressed in green,
She yet remains the beauty queen.

All through summer, tall and proud,
She stands there, regal, head unbowed.
The birds make nests among her leaves,
And she remains the queen of trees.

Then in September, changes start,
Yet still her beauty won't depart;
For now she's clothed in red and gold,
Till winter comes and takes a hold.

It throttles her – her leaves turn brown,
And now she feels a naked clown.
She stops pretending, lets them go,
Then bows her head with naught to show.

Beauty & Appreciation

She cannot bear to feel the shame;
Sleeping helps to dull her pain.
She dreams of all her former glory...
Incomplete is yet her story.

Winter, meanwhile, changed its mind,
Repented; now it's being kind.
It dresses her in silver ice,
And not just once, but really twice.

So, though sleeping, she stands proud;
Demands respect from all around.
And finally, though the ice may melt,
Still a pretty card she's dealt.

For spring returns, and now is seen
The glory of our great Snow Queen.
Her boughs again are clothed in white,
And now we see her beauty right.

A Welcome Storm

The rain, a-drumming on the roof,
Makes a homey sound.
And, while falling, cools the air,
And soaks the dried-out ground.

The wind that blows, though violently,
Is really welcome too.
It blows against my face and arms
And feels so nice and cool.

So, quite frankly, I must say,
I'm glad this storm arose.
It's cooled the air and made it fresh,
And cheered my tired nose.

A Raindrop's Tale

A raindrop am I; all my life have I lived
Rising and falling in many a place.
Still I remember, in days of my youth,
The time when the earth had no visible face.

The first time I fell in all of my life
Was during the flood – the great one, you know,
That killed all mankind but a few that God saved;
There I was, sorry to see the whole show.

'Twas many years later that deep in the desert,
No raindrops had fallen in many a year.
I heard a man call, "O Lord, let it rain!"
As quickly I fell there to land on his ear.

I fell on a boat one time, in a storm,
As the crew in hysterics their Master awoke.
When He, with a word, calmed the wind and the sea,
I knew Him, for I came to be when He spoke.

I've fallen in oceans, I've fallen in lakes.
I've fallen on ice in many a place.
If you could just listen, I'd tell such a tale –
'Til the time I evaporate, leaving no trace.

This poem was inspired by a silly story my brother told me, and is obviously fiction, but references, from a raindrop's perspective, several true biblical events. These include the faceless earth of Genesis 1:2, the flood of Genesis 7, the story of Elijah found in 1 Kings 18 and summarized in James 5:17, and finally the story of Jesus calming the storm, which is told in Matthew 8:23-27, Mark 4:35-41, and Luke 8:22-25.

Dream Garden

White roses, yellow roses,
Red roses and pink;
Nothing ever could be quite
As sweet as them, I think.

Peonies of red and white,
And every shade between,
Have such nice, thick petals
As to fit them for a queen.

Irises: purple, gold, and white,
Some blue, and some maroon;
How like heaven they all look,
This summer afternoon.

The Ice Cream Tulips in their place,
Pink with creamy white,
Look so realistic I'm
Inclined to try a bite!

This garden has such loveliness
I've never seen before.
How sad it is to know the truth
That dreams can last no more.

Gypsy Music

There is a rustling in the grass;
What is that sound I hear?
It sounds like someone walking,
Their footfalls very near.

Now I see, between the trees,
A young girl dressed in white.
A case she carries in her hand,
Her steps are soft and light.

She makes her way along the path
To a clearing in the woods.
There she opens up her case
And so reveals her goods.

It holds a violin which she removes
And tries a note.
She lifts it to her shoulder
And her song reveals her folk.

The piece she plays so beautifully
Goes by the name Czardaz.
She dimples in a lovely smile,
Enjoying the sound she plays.

Wow! Oh my! Her fingers fly
As she plays the fastest part;
But after a minute she slows down
And calms my racing heart.

Beauty & Appreciation

Now she plays, quite skillfully,
Such lovely, long, high notes.
I think the song is over;
My chest, it seems to float.

But then, no way! She's off again!
Once more her fingers fly!
How can she play this song so fast?
The complexity makes me cry!

At last, with a final long, sweet note,
The song is really done.
She puts the instrument in its case,
All lit with the setting sun.

And as she walks away, it seems
The birds don't sing as well.
That gypsy music is in my ears,
And so unforgettable!

I fell in love with the violin when I was too young to even remember, and took lessons for years. This poem was inspired by an actual music video by Webb Family Music. The first time I saw it was also the first time I had heard this piece, and these were really the feelings I experienced watching it.

Springtime Song

The sunshine warm upon my face,
The wind that calls to give it chase,
The sky so blue that one could gaze
Into its depths for days and days.

The fresh green smell borne on the wind,
The beauty of the world undimmed;
The flowers blooming on the green –
The beauty everywhere is seen.

I breathe in deeply; feel the thrill
As unknown voids at last are filled,
For ever through the winter long,
My heart did yearn for springtime song.

I skip from here to there and on –
My heart is full of happy song.
The trees at last are turning green,
And now a birdie starts to sing.

A kitten chasing butterflies,
The grass in which a daisy lies,
The rosebush putting forth its leaves;
Yes, everything is made to please.

The world, God made so beauty-full
That we might see His hand in all.
To think – that He would do all this
That I might know that I am blessed!

The Racetrack Rainbow

Bay, chestnut, gray and dun –
All of these colors still can run.
Color hasn't aught to do
With what kind of horse wins true.

Scarlet, green, violet, blue;
Stable colors running true.
All these colors dot the track
With the jockeys giving slack.

Their hooves pound, their noses blow;
The crowd's cheers seem to make them go.
Then, all at once, it's over and
The winner's decked in roses grand.

Bay, chestnut, gray and dun –
Out of them all, the fastest won.
Scarlet, green, violet, blue –
Just one of these a winner true.

My Garden

Daffodils, tulips, marigolds;
Many different shades of rose.
Aliums, violets, pansies dear,
'Round a pool of water clear.

Your nose smells, your eye sees
All these pretty things with ease.
You long to hold one in your hand;
I give you a bouquet so grand.

Autumn Beauty

The trees are clothed in red and gold
Instead of their summer green;
The sight of them this afternoon's
The prettiest I have seen.

Some leaves fall and dance around,
As playful as can be,
Twirling, fluttering, up and down,
All around the tree.

Those on the trees do tremble,
Anxious to join the ones
Who dance and skip and run and play,
All for the north wind's fun.

Soon they'll fall down to the earth,
Brown, unwanted and dull
To be trampled by uncaring feet,
Then buried in snow like wool.

Until that day of sorrow comes,
Enjoy now, while you may,
The sight of autumn beauty,
So entrancing while it stays.

Path of Life

Prisoners of White

Gently falling from the sky
Are snowflakes soft and white.
They pile up against the house;
They're shutting out the light!

We're now stuck inside the house,
My siblings four, and I,
Sipping cocoa by the fire
And eating home-baked pie.

We prepare to eat Thanksgiving dinner
Alone, by candlelight.
For we are still locked in by snow,
The prisoners of white.

We have no turkey, duck, or goose,
For which we may give thanks.
But we feel just as grateful for
Our good old roast goat shanks.

We didn't pick our pumpkins yet,
So, no pumpkin pie…
But we've got some spaghetti squash
To use without a sigh.

We haven't got the popcorn yet,
So we must go without;
But count our blessings just the same –
That's what it's all about!

We sit down to our simple meal,
Thanksgiving in our hearts,
Grateful for the warmth and food
And family by our hearth.

Path of Life

Oh, the Beauty of Winter!

Have you looked out the window?
The beauty outside beckons.
The snow outside is blinding bright;
The winter has awakened.

The snow is always beautiful,
But here is something more.
The trees, enrobed in shimmery silver,
Shine like never before.

The branches, bare, were dark and dull
As late as yesterday,
But now, under burdens of crystalline ice,
They shine in a marvelous way.

Looking, you can't keep your breath;
In an instant, it's taken away.
The beauty of all God's creation,
So poignant and fresh in this way.

Oh, the beauty of winter!
Oh, the ice on the trees!
Oh, how fresh and how clean the air
In spite of the chill in the breeze!

The sun, coming out of a sudden,
Contributes the final touch.
And to no one's surprise
The beauty surpasses much.

Beauty & Appreciation

The ice shines brighter than ever
Like silvery Christmas lights;
And the sun goes dark again
As daytime turns to night.

Path of Life

The West is on Fire!

The west is on fire!
All red is the sky
With tinges of pink
And golden up high.

White clouds to the north
Turn loveliest pink;
The rest of the sky is
So blue I must blink.

The eastern horizon
Is green – but the west?
It's on fire, I say!
The view there is best.

The west is on fire!
Once more hear my cry.
Though now I can sense
That it's starting to die.

The pink clouds turn white,
The red west turns blue,
And now, day is done;
The sun said adieu.

God's Evening Cure

The soft breeze blows my cares away
And the moon lights up the dark,
While the soft rain washes tears away
And erases sorrow's mark.

I take a deep breath of the cool country air;
A different emotion I feel.
First a small smile, then a tiny laugh,
And last all at once a great peal!

Evening Peace

The purring of a kitty cat,
The cheery little crickets' chat,
The shining of the silver moon,
They sing a pretty evening tune.

The soft, delightful evening breeze,
The pigeons cooing in the trees,
The bright stars twinkling in the sky,
They make me heave a happy sigh.

The smell of freshness in the air,
The breeze that's tugging at my hair,
The feel of nighttime harmony;
It seems God made them all for me.

The rain that starts to touch my face,
The small frogs talking in their place,
The whispering of the trees, it seems,
Says to all, "Good night, sweet dreams!"

The smell of peace is strong tonight;
It's close to the silver moon so bright.
Yes, every raindrop carries peace.
It comes with every breath of breeze.

The peace I feel right here is more
Than all I've ever felt before.
The only reason I have found
Is that God's handiwork's around.

A Cold, Clear Night

The air is clear and crisp and cold;
I'm filled with joy, a hundredfold!
For I can see the stars tonight
And for once, the moon is bright.

The last few nights were cloudy, so
One could not see the moonlight show.
Those nights were windy too, and cold;
Bitterly so, if you've been told.

This night, though chilly, is pretty too.
The stars are not a motley crew!
I gaze up at the sky and know –
I'm happy in the silver glow.

The Pretty Blue Moon

The pretty blue moon is shining,
Lighting a path through the trees.
The pretty blue moon is lighting
A world that is cooled by a breeze.

The pretty blue moon's a late riser;
It rarely is seen before night.
The pretty blue moon is yet nicer,
And oh, such a beautiful sight!

The pretty blue moon's a delight;
The sight takes my breath away!
The pretty blue moon is a light
To those who may wander astray.

III.

Life, Faith, Relationship

Life, Faith, Relationship

Half Past Thirteen

At the age of twelve, life starts to change.
I never knew what hit me, but it was strange!
My feelings are different, my life is a mess!
I'm confused every day, and sad, more or less…

I don't know what to do; *some*body help me!
I'm confused, and unhappy, and grumpy, you see.
I'm tired, and lonely, and so badly need *touch!*
I'm grounded from phone calls for talking too much.

What would I do in the next year, two, or three
If it weren't for my friend who is older than me?
So much is changing – my body, my life…
What can I do with this difficult strife?

I'm very confused 'bout my looks and my friends
And I've no extra time to tie up the loose ends.
I want to ride horses; I feel so left out!
And frequently feel that I can't hide a pout!

Nowadays I sometimes feel ready to cry
When before I'd not even have batted an eye.
I can't think a mite, and I don't know a thing;
Sometimes I feel crazy at half past thirteen.

What Do You See?

What do you see when you look at the sun?
I see a masterpiece made by Someone.
Created to see by, to keep us all warm –
And still for some purpose, for something much more.
What was it made for? To help us to see,
But not earthly things – no, there's more yet to be!

What do you see when you look at the stars?
I see a zillion beacons afar.
How many sweet indications of grace
Are hung in the skies, bringing joy to my face!
What were they made for? To help us to see.
But what? Not the skies! For there's more yet to be.

What do you see when you look at the sea?
I see an image of love, oh so deep.
A display of great power, and yet somehow calm,
For even its tempests are held in A Palm.
What was it made for? To help us to see.
But what? Not just water! There's more yet to be!

What do you see when you look at the trees?
A picture of growth, of health to be seen.
A strong limb or willowy – all are the same.
How so? They all were created by name.
What were they made for? To help us to see.
Just foliage? Nay, for there's more yet to be.

Life, Faith, Relationship

What do you see when you look at the hills?
I see a majesty needing no frills.
With grass and with flowers, abundantly clothed;
Just see how their beauty is plain to behold!
What were they made for? To help us to see.
The beauty of earth? No, there's much more to be!

I could yet go on; I could prattle and rave
Of forests and tigers and bears in their caves.
I could go into detail on bees and their hives
Or try to do justice to rainbows and skies,
But what were they made for? You've heard it enough!
One more, then I'll tell you what's meant by this stuff.

What do you see when you look at a child?
I see an image of beauty so wild!
Someone created a person to be
His special friend, and uniqueness unseen.
Yes, we are the crown of all that He made!
We are His joy, made never to fade.

We are the final, the favorite, the best.
We are all that He cared to call blessed.
Yet somehow, we lost it… forgot it… we fell.
Fell away from His bosom, away from the Well.
His life cannot reach us, so far have we gone;
We've lost our nature to always belong.

Path of Life

We lost the relationship, lost all our hope.
Lost the great life that He gave, and we mope.
We long for Home, for the sacred place
Where fear won't exist, and True Love's commonplace.
What was it all made for? To help us to see…
To see that a God made it all to be seen!

Creation, created by God for our joy –
It's there all around us! It lifts up its voice,
Singing praise, giving glory to God in His place.
It lifts Him up, calls us to see His kind face.
So turn, join the song; sing to Jesus alone!
For Him was created this glorious throne!

My Love For You

My child, if you but knew the agony gone through;
My act of love unrivaled as I went to Hell for you.
If you could comprehend what deep desire kept Me there,
At the last extent of pain yet with the bliss of Heaven to bear –
If you could just imagine what that moment was to Me,
You'd know then how unquenchable My love will ever be.

You were the joy before Me when I felt a friend betray;
The reason that I held My peace when I had much to say.
You were the one I thought of in the mockery and pain,
And you alone could keep Me there when Father turned away.
You still were My delight as I descended into Hell –
To death's defeat resounding in a deep and final knell!

If only you could know My love, you'd never be the same.
You are My one desire, the one I long to claim.
Dear heart, would you just turn to Me and give to Me your all?
My arms are here to hold you, My ears to hear your call.
My love for you could never fail, I promise nothing less,
But simply ask that you would give Me all of you – your best.

Flash Flood in My Heart

Warning! There's a flash flood
Deep inside my heart!
This sounds as though it would be bad,
But it's an awesome start!

My heart was parched and dry;
The heat I could not stand.
The hate, the fear, the grief, the pain –
They gripped me by the hands.

Deep regret and shame, all over
Things I can't undo;
I knew I'd been forgiven,
Yet how could it be true?

Then Abba sent a flash flood
Of love inside my heart.
Washed away the grief and shame
And gave me a new start.

The rain is pouring down,
The love is washing out
The dirt and grime inside my heart
And love is shining out!

All but the foundation,
Everything must go.
The filthy, weed-filled topsoil
So now good things can grow!

Life, Faith, Relationship

Gardener and Father, my Best Friend –
We'll never be apart.
Thank You, God, for sending me
A flash flood in my heart!

I was inspired to write this by an actual heavy rainstorm after a drought; the rain and the washing away of the soil was something I actually witnessed. As I sat on the fence with the rain soaking my body from every side and the entire ground covered in running water, I knew I could use it as a beautiful illustration. By the way, the name "Abba" is Hebrew for Father.

My Calling

There is a life I'm called to lead,
And not like any other;
A great commission just for me,
Unmatched by any other.

There is a path I'm called to take
Which none has trod before,
And none will ever follow me
In life or ever more.

Some together twist and wind,
And maybe for a while,
But no two ever are the same
For every single mile.

I cannot look on others' lots
And wonder how they be;
For I have my own life to live
And my own path to see!

I have a Guide whom I must know,
A faith I must not lose.
A will to follow on and on,
A strength to rightly choose.

A trust in God who will not fail,
A love just like His own.
A reason to survive and thrive
Is mine when He is home.

Life, Faith, Relationship

So as I walk in my own way,
According to the Word,
And keep quite clear of wishing for
Another type of world,

I will find fulfillment then,
In every single day,
As I walk out my calling
According to the Way.

Path of Life

In the Shadow of His Hand

Though enemies attack me
Day and night from every land,
I am safe and I'm protected
In the shadow of His hand.

Though my life is filled with war
Against the Evil One's dark band,
I find comfort, I find peace,
In the shadow of His hand.

Although the enemy tries his best
To steal the joy at hand,
I find happiness and strength
Inside the shadow of His hand.

So, though the enemy tries to
Take away my faith, I can
Turn to God, who'll give me strength,
In the shadow of His hand.

Even if my friends should turn,
And tell me not to stand,
I'll find the strength to keep it up
In the shadow of His hand.

This title and theme come from a book I read by the same name, about a Holocaust survivor named Anita Dittman. It was one of my favorite books around that time, and I was as fascinated as Anita by the idea of being kept in the shadow of God's hand.

Psalm 23

My shepherd is God;
What more do I need?
If my Father's the king,
I am free indeed.

He provides for me pastures,
Greener than green;
My paths stay close
To peaceful streams.

My strength is renewed;
In His presence I'll stay.
In righteous paths
I am guided each day.

To bring glory to His Name,
He shows me what's right.
Though in dark valleys
And wand'ring by night,

Why should I fear?
You're close by my side.
In the shadow of Your garments
I find room to hide.

Your rod and staff
Will protect me, I know.
No enemy dares to remain
Where You go.

Path of Life

A table is loaded
With food for Your lamb.
It's placed in the center
Of the enemy's camp.

You pour oil on my head
To anoint me, O Lord,
So that I may do
What You point me toward.

My cup overflows
With everything good,
And my heart with thanksgiving
As always it should.

Your goodness and mercy
Will never stop coming,
Following even when
From You I'm running.

I'll live in Your house
For all eternity,
There out of reach
Of my soul's enemy.

The title says it all; this is based on Psalm 23. However, to make it come alive more and work rhythmically and rhyme, I did throw some extra ideas in that aren't part of the psalm.

Life, Faith, Relationship

Help Me

Help me, Lord, to keep my eyes
And my thoughts on You.
Oh, it is so hard sometimes;
I know You know 'tis true.

Help me be undistracted
By the world around today.
Help me focus on You, God;
The Life, the Truth, the Way.

Help me choose You, my Best Friend;
You're always there, I know.
Abba, Father, stay with me,
And help me You to know.

This poem contains a reference to the words of Jesus in John 14:6, as well as the use of the Hebrew word "Abba," meaning "Father."

The Only Good Thing

The world's gone kinda crazy,
And as I look around,
I realize there's a problem,
And so many have drowned.

I listen to the news,
But it's all lost on me.
The only thing I understand is
You're the only good I see.

The only good thing I can find,
The only good thing I can see.
The only good thing all around,
But God, You are enough for me.

Everything that's beautiful,
And everything You made;
They distort and alter it,
And make true beauty fade.

But there's one thing they cannot change,
And that one thing is You.
You always stay the same;
Your word is always true.

They try to hide You from us,
Replace You in the schools.
They try to say that faith in You
Simply isn't "cool."

Life, Faith, Relationship

But if I be a Noah,
Why should I ask more?
'Cause You're the best thing in my world,
The One worth living for!

God, You're the best thing I can find,
The best of all that I can see.
You're the best thing all around,
And far more than enough for me.

Path of Life

Little By Little

I feel lost in a wilderness I didn't enter.
I feel trapped in a web I did not weave.
I try, but I cannot free myself.
I can't find the way to leave.

My wanderings take me deeper in,
My struggles tighten it more,
And the more that I try to free myself,
The deeper the lifelong sores.

I'm sinking 'neath the surface; someone pushed me in.
I'm falling off a mountain I never even climbed.
I try to rise to the surface,
But the waves come every time.

The more I try to catch myself,
The faster that I fall.
The more I try to learn to swim,
The less I can at all.

What do I do when I can't get out?
What do I do when I'm stuck?
What do I do when I can't get my feet
Out of the horrible muck?

I turn to my friends, I turn to the world,
But my friends just pull me in.
The world is worse; it pushes
And then watches with a grin.

Life, Faith, Relationship

I go to church, I read the Word,
But I find nothing there.
I wonder why I feel so lonely,
Of all places, there?

But then I heard that someone said,
"God's presence changes naught.
Submission to God's presence, though,
That will change a lot."

So I listened and I thought,
"Well, it's worth a try.
If it doesn't work, however,
I would love to die."

So I surrendered all to God,
Gave Him my heart and will.
I ceased my struggles, trusted Him,
And I trust Him still!

Little by little, He guides me out
Of the wilderness so wild.
Little by little untangles the web,
While comforting me, His child.

Though I'm still in the wilderness,
Though I'm still stuck fast,
God is with me, and I can trust
In the One Who's first and last!

Path of Life

Though I'm still near drowning
And can't find solid ground,
There's a Hand below which bears me up
And a Presence all around.

So my struggling is no more;
I lie back and trust in Him
Who holds the waters in His hand
And teaches me to swim.

The concept of God delivering us little by little comes not only from personal experience; it is scriptural. One of the most encouraging verses I think I've ever read is Exodus 23:29-30; repeated in Deuteronomy 7:22-23. It says, "I will not drive [your enemies] out from before you in one year, lest the land become desolate and the wild beasts multiply against you. Little by little I will drive them out from before you, until you have increased and possess the land." (Exodus 23:29-30; please read the other verse too!!)

In other words, God knows about enemies we don't even know about, and He knows how ready we are for life. He manages our obstacles in His timing for our benefit because what we want (instant deliverance), in some cases would be really bad for us! When I read this verse, I took a walk and spent some time thinking about it and how it applied to my situation. I truly felt lost, trapped, and hopelessly entangled in problems I had nothing whatsoever to do with creating. I went home and wrote this poem, and I hope this biblical truth encourages you as it did me.

I Trust You

My heart is overflowing,
With what I can't explain.
All I know is it hurts so bad,
This never-ending pain.

My emotions are out of whack –
My thoughts give me such guilt –
Yet through the uncertainty,
Your love is with me still.

Love, expressed through joy,
Patience, kindness, and peace;
Your goodness and Your faithfulness
Are not the least of these.

Gentleness and self-control
Complete the list above;
These eight are the expressions of
Your pure and holy love.

I know that in the whirlwind
Caused by the enemy,
Father, You still love me
And You still speak to me.

Soft, I hear Your whisper;
Your voice fills me with peace:
"Daughter, I still love you."
I'm secure here in Your peace.

Path of Life

I hear and I obey;
I'll sing all through the storm,
And I'll talk to You
Though I'm tired and I'm worn.

And I'll dwell upon the things
That are holy, that are pure,
Lovely, righteous, just;
Such are worthy, I am sure.

"Whatever's worthy of praise"
You told me, and I will.
When all the world is ugly
I'll obey You still.

Because *You'll* still be left;
They can't take You away.
You always will be worthy,
To the end of all my days.

Abba, I trust You;
In Your shadow I will dwell.
A thousand may fall;
Ten thousand go to Hell –

But it shall not come near me,
My eyes alone will look,
To see the wicked treated
According to Your Book.

Life, Faith, Relationship

Like a palm tree, Lord, You said,
Will the righteous flourish;
The way of the ungodly, though,
Is known to always perish.

I will not fear the deceiver;
He cannot harm my soul.
His servants hurt my body,
But in Heaven I keep my gold.

The deceiver, he may toy with
My emotions and my thoughts,
And Father, You know!
He does it such a lot.

But He cannot take Your love;
Your peace remains with me.
I will not dwell upon the road
With its uncertainty.

My soul will rest in Your embrace;
I trust You with my life.
And I will keep my thoughts on You
Instead of on the strife.

This particular poem is just rich with scripture references! I will list them out so you can look them up if you so desire. The fruit of the Spirit (love expression) comes from Galatians 5:22-23. Philippians 4:8 tells us what to think about, Psalm 91:1, 7-8 talk about living in God's shadow and watching from safety as a thousand and ten thousand fall beside us, and Psalm 1:3, 6 refer to the flourishing of the righteous and perishing of the wicked.

My Story

I've known You, God, I thought so well.
I've felt Your touch each time I fell.
I knew that I was loved by You,
And I knew much about You too.

I trusted You through darkest days
And close beside You I had stayed.
I said that I would never leave;
I came to You with every grief.

What changed in me, so wont to kneel?
For I have lost my former zeal.
I yet recall, so recently,
When You were everything to me.

So much did change in all my life,
Yet You were there throughout the strife.
You showed me just the way to go;
You told me all that I need know.

And that was when the change was made –
My love for You began to fade.
How my heart breaks to say it now.
The gift before the Giver, how?

And yet, that's so, that's what I did.
Your words lost to another bid.
I gave my time and energy
To things I loved but selfishly.

Life, Faith, Relationship

I still looked good, and all I met
Said that Your love I did reflect,
But something they could never know
Is I was running really low.

I knew that all was not quite right;
Running on fumes, I knew the sight.
I knew I was headed for a crash
But still I was sure for a while I'd last.

"When I have a problem, I'll fix it," I said –
I knew in my heart 'twas a lie in my head.
My life was too comfy, and lazy was I.
"Far too much work to now change it," says I.

I was sharing my story, and everyone loved it.
But me, I just felt like a hypocrite.
It seemed like my story was over just then
For I knew not how it could go on again.

But oh, help me never to grow so content!
My story goes on; it is never past tense!
If I ever stop climbing then down I will fall.
I desire to never let go of it all.

Give us revival, and start it in me.
I ask You to change every part of me.
Do what You will; leave nothing untouched!
And change me not little. Oh God, change me much!

Path of Life

I regret to say that this has been my story multiple times over. It is a common one, but God is so good to take us back every time and show us the way to continue following Him closely again.

Path of Life

I tried to walk this path of life
Without You by my side;
I'd call on You now and again,
But it wasn't bona fide.

It wasn't easy, let me say;
And that's an understatement!
Many's the time when I would feel
All sad, alone, and spent.

I thought I had a faith in You
That always was sincere;
And yet I felt as if you were
A God who wasn't near.

I knew something was wrong with this,
But I couldn't pin it down.
I knew I needed something more,
But it could not be found.

I knew that You were real
But couldn't understand
How I could go to church each week
And never feel Your hand.

Now I know that I was sleeping,
Always unaware.
I didn't know that I was missing
You just everywhere.

Path of Life

Like one who sleeps and doesn't know
The house is burning down;
The one who doesn't smell the smoke
While others run around.

Calmly sleeping, peacefully,
Dreaming all is well,
And trusts in water miles off
While on the way to Hell.

But I began to feel the heat;
My room began to flame.
You came into my dreams just then
And softly spoke my name.

And hallelujah, I woke up!
Then, petrified, I stared.
The flames came ever closer 'round,
And oh, how I was scared.

My eyes began to sting and burn,
My lungs were filled with smoke.
I beat at the fire with a dirty rag
And cursed the night I woke.

And though I fought with all my might,
The flames crept ever close.
At last I dropped my rag and watched
The flames that licked my toes.

Life, Faith, Relationship

All hope was gone; I sat and sobbed
While soot turned black my face.
But when I saw You standing there
The flames moved back a pace.

While they yet burned so close to me
You wrapped me in Your arms.
You whispered words of comfort;
Your voice was soft and warm.

The danger wasn't past though, and
So after calming me,
You asked if I would fight the fire,
"Hand in hand with Me."

I answered, "Lord, I think it's hopeless,
But if You say it's not,
I'll trust in You, and I will follow
Though the flames be hot."

And now I walk this path of life
Every day with You.
I realize You were always there
Though I overlooked You.

You don't fix all my problems;
My life is not that easy.
I'm saying, life is hard;
Harder even, maybe.

Path of Life

The difference is You're with me.
My hand is clasped in Yours.
Your peace is always with me
Though the storm around me roars.

And when I am confused,
I do not have to fret,
For You will always guide me;
My needs are always met.

So as I walk this path of life
I'll stay close by Your side.
The thought of living it alone
I simply can't abide.

I'll follow You through every storm,
I'll trust You in the fire.
Please help me to never change my mind,
But to follow You still higher.

This truly is my story; I was a confused, lukewarm Christian going to church because of my parents' faith. When God caught my attention, it was only just in time. I can't imagine how I would have navigated the following years of my life without Him; I would certainly be a different person even if I came out alright in the end, and I'm not certain I would have. My gratefulness to the Lord and my church cannot be expressed, for turning me to Him just in time before my life burned down.

Love of My Life

Oh! The joy! I'm bursting at the seams!
I've found the love I always thought was only in my dreams!
The overflow of Jesus' love, the peace that washes me;
I never thought it'd really be so deep, so pure, *so free!*

I want to dance and sing! I want to laugh and weep!
I want to feel it all the time; I never want to sleep!
I feel that I could fly, I can't hold back the tide!
I simply can't describe to you this welling deep inside!

Sitting on the couch, I heard a worship song.
Only in a whisper I began to sing along.
"There's nothing like Your love" were the only words I said;
For then I could but sit and feel, so tenderly was I held!

I felt the Father's loving arms, wrapped 'round all of me.
I felt the love, the perfect peace, so very tangibly.
With nothing else to think about, love was all I felt.
I heard the music, nothing else, as in His presence I dwelt.

I wished that I could stay and that the moment wouldn't end.
But of course, it had to, though as God did intend.
I feel His love *inside* me now; He'll never let me go.
I know, as sure as that I breathe, with me He'll ever go.

God is King, my Lover, my Friend, and my Prince of Peace.
When I'm in trouble, He draws me close, and sets my heart at ease.
When I feel lost I know He's there, and He will be my Guide.
And when I'm lonely, still He's close, a Best Friend true and tried.

Path of Life

When fleshly desires try to break in, unhealthy in all the worst ways,
I turn my eyes upon Jesus, and He's my desire each day.
The only one I can always confide in, in every little thing...
My Savior, Foundation, Love of my Life, of Him I forever will sing!

This is a completely true story; it actually happened just as it says. I was sitting on the couch with worship music playing in the house, and during a song I had never yet liked (Where You Are by Leeland), I whispered the words "There is nothing like Your love" and God's presence immediately overwhelmed me. This was truly my first reaction; I wrote this poem just after the moment ended. And that song now always brings back that lovely memory.

My Hands

Thank You, God, for my two hands;
I can do many things with them.
I cook, play music, write words and
Pluck a flower from its stem.

I fix my clothes, I brush my hair,
I color pretty things.
I really do more with my hands
Than one could ever dream!

But two things I do with my hands
That I must never cease:
I fold my hands in prayer and
I lift them high in praise.

The Cry of My Heart

Thank You, dear Lord,
For amusements and fun.
Thank You for food
And warmth from the sun.

Thank You for friends,
And family, too.
Thank You for eyes,
And ears to hear You.

Thank You for pets
To brighten our days,
And thank You for lips,
That we might sing praise.

But the gifts I most desire,
God, to thank You for today
Are the talents and abilities
You gave me for Your way.

I'm grateful You made me
To write poetry.
Thank You so much
Just for making me *me!*

Please help me to use it
To glorify You.
All else that I ask is
To help others, too.

Life, Faith, Relationship

I do not want glory
Or money or fame;
I want to help others
To realize this same:

That there is no other
Except You who can
Satisfy them in
Their greatest demand.

The one demand
They don't understand:
That emptiness
Inside of each man.

There's only One
Who can fill the void –
At each right step
He's overjoyed!

God, help me to use
My words to show
The one thing
Everyone should know.

Just grant me this –
That's all I pray,
And that You would help me
Never to stray

Path of Life

From the task You gave us,
To tell everyone
Of Your great love,
And what You have done.

This is my cry,
The cry of my heart,
To tell the whole world
That they're dear to Your heart.

It Could Have Been

There's one place you must never go,
If ever you'd succeed:
A wasteland called *It Could Have Been*;
Now listen and take heed.

For this place does look so fair
When you look in from out;
It lies so very close at hand
Where'er you go about.

To tempt you always to go in,
To be ensnared by doubt,
To sigh for how it could have been,
And leave the world without.

If you should stray into this land
Along the path of thought,
You'd find it hard to get back out,
For doubt would have you caught.

You'd be quite sure reality
Would never measure up,
And with the words, "if only"
You'd always interrupt.

"If only it were different!"
"If only it wasn't so!" –
And yet if it were not,
You'd wish it were, you know!

Path of Life

Do yourself a favor:
Avoid, however fair,
All thoughts of how it could have been –
Let others wander there.

Dreams and Fantasy

Many things go through my head,
Good and bad, so much is said.
I stand and dream and no one knows
What fantasy inside me grows;
And constantly my dreams are fed.

Many things go on, you see,
These little dreams, and fantasy.
They take up far, far too much time,
And now I know, for 'tis no rhyme:
My thoughts have all but conquered me.

What shall I do? What can I say
To make it all just go away?
What happened that I lost control?
Can't a person own one's soul?
Oh, but what an evil day!

I say, cannot the Truth be found?
Why am I by thoughts held bound?
I know 'tis true, I understand
That I must take Him by the hand,
Yet still temptation's all around.

It's simply choice, decisiveness –
The first step up to find success.
Decide for all time ne'er to succumb,
Then lean on Him who's overcome,
And know that by Him I am blessed.

Poison in My Mind

All day long I watch my screen –
Play dumb games, scroll online.
All day long, I watch and listen
But it's poison to my mind.

All night long in bed I watch
The content made and slayed online;
All night long my brain is rotting,
Taking poison to my mind.

All day long my ears are filled
With the voices found online;
All day long consuming junk and
Taking poison to my mind.

Oft I wish to stop and think,
But all these voices, found online,
Give me reason to believe
There's naught but poison in my mind.

There's no reason I should think
All for myself, with facts online.
Oh, they're breaking me by stages,
Feeding poison to my mind.

There's no way for me to know
What is true or false online.
All I know is nothing's left
To me but poison in my mind.

What is Emotion?

What is emotion? A thing in the wind.
Sometimes it makes me want to sin.
Sometimes it's pleasant, but oftentimes mean.
Often it makes me wish not to be seen.

Emotions cause trouble, forbidding tact.
When I want to wait, they press me to act.
They cause me to fear what people think;
Sometimes I wish through the floor to sink!

Emotions confuse me and sometimes hurt.
Emotions are painful, but how can they hurt?
How can they – unseen, and touching me not –
Hurt me so much or turn my face hot?

Emotions are painful – difficult, too.
They make me forget what I ought to do…
But really now, wouldn't our lives be dull
If we had no emotions in life at all?

Someday Perhaps

How many times I've looked at you
And thought of all I wished I knew;
I've wondered, could it come to be
That I'm with you and you're with me?

Each time you walk into the room
My heart jumps up and makes a boom.
My day is brighter, all at once;
You're all it takes to meet my wants.

We talk, and how you make me laugh!
And oh, the fun we often have!
There's so much others do not know
That you and I both love and so

It seems our lives are well aligned,
Yet is it planned by God on high?
I wish I knew the answer, but
Until I do, my mouth is shut.

And so I watch you secretly,
And at times, so jealously,
And wonder when I'll ever see
If one our lives are meant to be.

I know I cannot call you "dear,"
And yet such words I long to hear
And say, but wait, just wait... Someday,
Perhaps those words I'm meant to say.

Life, Faith, Relationship

This is the only really "romantic" poem I've ever written because I work very hard to control my thoughts and follow the Lord's will instead of fantasizing about relationships I'm not meant to have. This illustrates quite clearly what goes on inside my head when I know someone who seems a likely fit and whose character and personality I find attractive though I still have no direction from God regarding him.

Mark Upon My Heart

If you and I have ever met,
If we've exchanged a word
Or even just a look or two
Without it being heard.

If our gazes met across the room
Or if we've been good friends;
If our paths crossed for an instant
Or were joined until the end;

No matter if we've truly met
Or if we merely waved,
You've left a mark upon my heart
And I have many saved.

If you were good or bad to me,
Or you were simply there;
If you ignored or smiled at me,
It's surely true, I swear.

Whether 'twas on purpose
Or an accident, I'm sure,
You've left a mark upon my heart
That never can be cured.

And so, if e'er I meet you,
Be you friend or no,
Be kind enough to greet me,
To smile and say hello.

Life, Faith, Relationship

This heart of mine is delicate;
Your actions all will shape me.
I cannot control it;
Your unkindnesses will break me.

I know I need some help in life,
And your kind words will boost me;
Or even just a smile,
What a blessing that would be!

There's so much you could never know
And much you cannot change,
But each encouragement will leave
A hope for better days.

And how much time is left to us
Not one of us can know;
So now, before it gets too late –
Right now, let your love show.

Can I Trust Again?

How can life go on again?
Can I trust again?
Can I find a friend once more
After what has been?
My friend, I thought, who cared for me,
Has all my trust betrayed.
And no one is reliable,
And none has ever stayed.

How can life go on again?
Can I trust again?
Can I trust in heroes true
After what has been?
Someone I've always looked up to
Has fallen hard and fast.
Their life was all a lie, it seems,
From first until the last.

How can life go on again?
Can I trust again?
Can I ever feel safe or loved
After what has been?
For now, my dearest bosom friend,
I saw as pure and strong,
And thought I knew so well,
At last, has proven me all wrong.

Life, Faith, Relationship

Oh God, can life go on again?
Can I still trust again?
Though men may fall and all seem lost,
You're where You've always been.
Your arms are steady 'round me now,
Your heart is pressed to mine.
You hurt with me, and more besides,
Yet You are always mine.

This Shallow Life

You flit about with energy
Much more than I am wont to see;
You chatter like a guinea bird
As everyone around you heard.

You seem quite happy all the time
But I can see it's just a lie.
Your thoughts are clearly dangerous;
Your life is dark and, well, anxious.

You talk about such random things;
Your friends or all these ugly memes.
Your life, I see, is but a plague;
Your heart and mind are lost and vague.

Your days are filled with noise and speed –
All surface things, all meager feed.
This shallow life surrounds the core
Locked deep inside, which longs for more.

Your mind will never let you rest;
Your inner soul but sleeps at best,
While physically you toss and turn,
Your life a pain at every turn.

You'll never know while this goes on,
What 'tis that deep inside you longs;
For deep within you just want peace,
And true connection made at ease.

Life, Faith, Relationship

You know not what, but something more –
That will bring meaning to your core.
Something real, for once, and true;
Not these shallow, mocking clues.

Depression's hidden in your eyes,
For all around you've realized
This world's a fake and nothing's real,
So you pretend it makes you feel,

And, scared lest anyone should find
The real you hidden deep inside,
You make this confident persona;
All will hear your lovely mantra!

But I see you for who you are:
A broken, hurting, human heart.
Just know, I'm always here for you,
And I will keep on praying, too.

Something Missing

There's something missing in your life
Though you don't know what it is.
Maybe it's subconsciously
You try to solve the quiz.

There's something missing in your life
Every single day.
You try to find a remedy,
You try each likely way.

You try to fill the emptiness
That plagues your life with fun.
Or maybe you try to fill the gap
With work you must get done.

Maybe you try music,
Maybe games or dance.
Maybe, in delirium,
You try to find romance.

None of these will ever work,
Not one of them can fill
The natural hole in your life
That drives you toward the kill.

This gap can only ever be filled
By one, who'll stop the strife.
One Person who waits for permission to act,
To give you the breath of life.

Life, Faith, Relationship

Without Him there is no reason to live,
No reason to do anything.
Without Him you can't not feel empty;
I'm speaking of God, your King.

He is the one who made you.
He cares, oh, so deeply about you.
Turn to Him in your hour of need.
He cannot help but to love you!

If you truly have a relationship
With the One Who sets you free,
You'll feel as whole and complete
And yes, as content as could possibly be.

The Hidden Truth

As we talk, you smile and laugh,
And say you're doing fine.
But the more I listen to you,
The more I can see you're lying.

The more you smile too brightly,
The more it becomes quite plain.
Your outward laughter and ready smile
Are a mask for inner pain.

As much as you try to hide it,
I can see it in your eyes.
The makeup and the fancy clothes
Cannot make truth of lies.

Your eyes are full of pain;
They despairingly say,
"There is no solution.
My pain is here to stay.

"No one can help my trouble;
No one can make me glad.
There's no remedy for the tears I cry
At night, alone and sad.

"I've tried it all; what is the use
Of living anymore?
I'll never more be happy;
I'm desperate to the core.

Life, Faith, Relationship

"As long as I'm with people,
I'll smile and say I'm fine.
I do not wish to trouble them
With knowing I'll soon be dying.

"Then later, when I get home,
Convinced they do not care,
I'll decide to make the final move;
Into the mirror I'll stare…

"Then after a minute of doing so,
I'll leave my troubles behind.
I'm sure they do not love me.
I'm sure they will not mind."

All this I see inside your eyes –
In spite of all you say.
I must tell you something.
Wait, don't go away!

Believe it or not, I know Someone
Who takes the pain away.
Truly, unless He's in your life,
There is no reason to stay.

Without Him, life is truly worthless –
But He'll show His purpose to you.
He knows you better than you know yourself
Because He created you!

Path of Life

He made you, love, for a reason.
That should be enough.
Although, as I know too,
Life will still be rough.

But there's no need to worry;
He's overcome the world.
So though reality does mean pain,
He'll give you joy, sweet girl.

I have a lifelong friend who became suicidal in high school, and I wrote this about her. It is such a common thing though! If only we would take the time to truly see where people really are more often.

Life, Faith, Relationship

I Want the Real You Back

Though I hate to do it, I've got to ask:
What's underneath the makeup and mask?
You once had true beauty, which now you lack.
I want the real you back.

Once you were happy every day.
You'd smile and laugh 'most all the way.
What'll it take to change you back?
I want the real you back.

Now I watch you suffer; oh, horror! 'Tis true.
Each pain in your eyes makes me suffer too.
Each time I see you, a twist of the rack.
I want the real you back!

It's not pain to know what the pain is you've got;
The pain's to see you suffer, the reason know *not!*
Oh, how I long to help you turn back;
I want the real you back.

This isn't you; I know it is not!
I understand you've changed a lot,
But God can give you what you lack.
I want the real you back.

The way you dress, the way you act;
It all has changed, and that's a fact.
I love you. Come, get back on track!
I want the real you back.

Fight or Acquiesce

'Tis an ugly world we live in
And evil's at every turn.
Is it good or is it evil
For which your heart does yearn?

You either embrace it or fight it;
There is no other way.
You cannot sit on the fence
Pondering half the day.

And you can't say you don't know
If a thing is good or bad.
Does it point to none but Jesus
Or is it only a passing fad?

We must be far above reproach
Since the world's so evil!
How can we be examples
If our lives are full of filth?

Why, you are no better than your neighbor!
Is it righteous 'cause you don't go *quite* as far?
Is it suddenly okay because you hid it?
How can you say you never even did it?
You think but don't do, listen but don't see,
Yet as a person thinks inside, so is he.

So either fight or acquiesce,
And if you're sinning, why hold back?
The one thing's just as bad as all the other!
But if you'll choose to fight, I say,
Take heart! You're not alone.
God is on your side, you know, and He's already won!

One final word I'll leave with you,
Encouragement you'll need.
For those of you who choose the right,
'Twill be a fight indeed.

But when your friends all say you're weird,
When you feel left out;
When worse things yet do happen you,
Lift up your head and shout!

There's One who says, "I'm proud of you"
Each time to flesh you die.
Your Father in Heaven is proud of you,
And, dear one, so am I.

In many ways, honestly, I wrote this as a reminder for myself. We cannot be perfect; we are all and will always be sinful. And there's no difference in the guilt of one sin versus another; according to God's Word if you break one part of the law, you're guilty of all of it. But the key, for me, is fighting.

Many times God has reminded me that the important thing is that I haven't given in and said, "Okay, fine, I can't win, so I'm just going to give up and accept that I tend to sin in this way." That is the issue at hand: where is your heart? Have you stopped trying because you can't be perfect, or do you continue doing everything with your best effort, wholeheartedly as unto the Lord? I fail, of course. There are seasons where I give in for a time. But although I can't win, I know that fighting again and doing my best is all I can do in this life, and one day there will be a reward.

It Matters Not What Others Think

I will not change to please others;
I'll not try to be like the rest.
Most people don't get the message,
But God's way is always best.

I will not wear popular styles
Just 'cause people say they're the best.
Whatever you say I will not believe
In running around half-dressed.

In the world of music and movies,
Deviation from godliness stinks.
Today's entertainment is awful,
No matter what others may think.

Again, I won't talk like my friends;
Too often they curse and swear;
At best, all the negative comments
And hurt make me tear out my hair!

What matters it if people think
I'm crazy in the head?
What matters it if they believe
I'm weird, stuck up, not led?

It matters not one whit to me
What others have to say.
I'll follow God and Him alone
Until my final day.

"I Will Not Compromise"

Shema! An important word I teach,
Though our culture it defies.
Instead of "go with the flow"
I say, "I will not compromise."

Does this sound foreign to you, my friend?
Well, try it on for size.
What we need most is one who says,
"I will not compromise."

When one says, "I know it's wrong,
But just this once or twice."
One finds it harder later to say,
"I will not compromise."

What we need is the teen who looks
Temptation in the eyes,
And, quiet but firm, declares the word,
"I will not compromise."

If one stands still then more will join,
Though the enemy always lies,
"You'll be alone, if ever you say,
'I will not compromise.'"

But when you, with conviction strong,
Refuse to compromise,
Perhaps 'twill help another to say,
"I will not compromise."

If people would their Creator please,
And do what's right in His eyes,
Then they could say that simple, hard phrase,
"I will not compromise."

People care so much about
Looking good to human eyes,
They've forgotten that the word exists,
"I will not compromise."

Now, if you have listened to me,
Then friend, when temptations arise,
Remember my plea; draw courage to say,
"I will not compromise."

If something may not be right,
Then pause and realize
That if it's not found in God's word,
It would be compromise.

Make it your motto, make it a goal;
And now, for how time flies!
I'm sure you'll learn to embrace the phrase,
"I will not compromise."

And if you feel abandoned, know you're not alone.
Your Father says He's with you, and He never lies.
So listen for His whisper:
"I will *never* compromise."

The word "shema" is Hebrew and it means "listen!"

Appreciation

There's many dark clouds,
But if there were none
We would never fully
Appreciate the sun.

In the world there's much evil,
But if there was none
We would never fully
Appreciate God's Son.

This simple poem came from seeing the beautiful contrast between dark storm clouds and the bright sunshine.

Life, Faith, Relationship

A Lesson From the Shadows

I went outside and looked around,
And boy, was I surprised to see
That though the temp was fifty-three
And had been yesterday as well,
Still snow and ice lay on the ground,
Against the house, both safe and sound.

The sun was high, and strange it was;
For all around was warm and bright,
Yet in the shadows lingered white.
How could it be? It made no sense.
With sunshine warm so very nigh,
How could the ice still fail to die?

And so I stopped and thought it through.
Then said out loud, with eyes alight,
"I think I've read this riddle right!
Though God be in your life, it seems
He must be there in *every* thing;
Let not the shadows reign as king!"

And so it is, for as the sun
Must touch *each* place where shadows lay,
Let God be present every day!
The rubbish casts a shadow dark,
So throw it out – leave only light,
And let God burn away the night.

There isn't often snow in Texas, but when there is, the temperature often climbs quickly thereafter. This was a real revelation for me, and I

Path of Life

have marveled at the same phenomenon multiple times since documenting it in this beautiful poem.

Life, Faith, Relationship

Little Miss Sunshine

There was a girl I met one day,
Who once could run and jump and play,
Until a couple years ago
The poor girl's back was broken, so

The doctor said that she would be
A cripple all her life, you see.
This made her in anguish cry,
"Can I never again climb trees so high?"

It seemed her life was of no worth;
Never more could she run over the earth,
But after about a year or so
She learned the secret we all should know.

Now she's happy no matter what,
Though it seemed her door to joy was shut.
So, on her couch, she smiles away,
All day long and every day.

That's how she earned the nickname of,
"Little Miss Sunshine, happy dove."
People come to learn to smile,
From Little Miss Sunshine, happy child.

And now you see that joy is not
Based upon the life we've got.
Instead, we all must learn to live
In peace that God alone can give.

Path of Life

This is not a true story, but was inspired by two stories by Louisa May Alcott: the true story of her sister Beth, in Little Women, and a fictional story called Jack and Jill in which the girl, Jill, had a terrible back injury that prevented her from moving about.

Where Beauty Lies

The eye that loves you sees in you
Things that you will never see;
A beauty and imagined grace;
Something, perhaps, you'll never be.

The eye that knows you sees in you
Good things of which you're unaware.
Admiration stems from this,
And you may wonder why they care.

The eye indifferent sees in you
The closest to reality;
But somehow, still the furthest,
And some folks *will* see badly.

The eye that hates you sees in you
Things that simply don't exist.
A look and an imagined sneer,
And a deceptive ugliness.

Now I hope that you have learned
At least, that beauty lies
Not in how you really look,
But in the other's eyes!

So, good friend, here's my advice:
Be kind and do what's right.
If people love you then they will
See you in better light.

A Song of Good News

On a starlit night I think
Of all the places I could be,
But none of them seems quite as nice
As being on the plains, you see.
It is the best view of the stars,
Not blocked by houses, trees, or cars.
So I always wish to be
On the plains when stars are out,
Where there is no disrupting sound,
No spoken word, no muffled shout.

Far out in the lonely West,
I hear a voice begin to sing.
Not of stars, or girls, or dreams,
But of their Maker, Lord, and King.
One named Jesus, I now know,
Was born in a stable, long ago.
Think, a baby so important
That a star shone just to say,
"A baby now is born who
Will chase darkness clear away!"

Life, Faith, Relationship

Then, just to show how much he cared,
The baby's father, God,
Told some shepherds of His birth;
Not kings, but lowly shepherds trod
Their way to a stable, there to see
One born to die for you and me.
As for the star that shone for Him,
Its purpose wasn't looks alone.
Some wise men who lived far away
Came, following the star that shone.

They brought Him gold and frankincense,
And myrrh, a precious spice,
And worshiped Him on bended knee,
Their actions quite precise.
In awe I hear this story sweet;
So lovely my heart skips a beat.
But still, I wonder, how could He
Be so important that
A star shone to announce His birth –
That reason seems so flat.

Then I hear: when He grew up,
Great miracles He did.
He healed the sick and raised a man
Who in a grave had hid.
In a storm He walked on water;
From the dead raised Jairus' daughter.
All these things He did and more;
"A prophet, then," I thought,
"But still, of all the prophets, why
Was this *one* man worth such a lot?"

But finally the tale was told –
And what a story, my!
He, though nothing had done wrong,
Was forced at last to die!
The death of common criminals,
And worse, in fact, than animals.
And why? Because He spoke of love,
Forgiveness for His flock.
Because the law was not important
And He said, "I'm God."

Because He cared for sinful folk,
And called the "righteous" names;
Because His love for everyone
Could not be forced or tamed.
Because He was God's plan for us,
The enemy, who hated us,
Declared by killing Him he'd win,
And rule over the earth.
Just think if he had been quite right,
If vain had been God's birth!

But the Father had a plan,
And raised Him from the dead;
In trying to keep us from our God
The devil lost his head.
For all the keys to Heaven and Hell
Belong to Jesus now, they tell,
And we can have relationship
With God, all on our own.
And we can come to Him each day
And never be alone.

Life, Faith, Relationship

At last it all makes sense to me,
And now I understand.
If only I could be with Jesus now,
And hold His hand!
Ah, but when I leave this world,
I'll be with Him; it's in His Word.
And all this time can feel Him near
And ask Him for His help today
And live with Him for all my life;
For now I know this is the Way.

Path of Life

The Story for the Story

Every story has a story,
Every rhyme a reason.
Every song a history,
And every wind a season.

Every painting, every picture
Came from someone's inspiration.
If not for thought and planning,
Now, we would not have a nation.

Each building had an architect,
Each movie a producer;
And you think it was so different
In the making of the muser?

Does it take so much to think
Of how the thinker came to be?
If my shoes had a designer
Then who created me?

Who gave me thought to think today
Of how it all exists?
Who made it so that I could find
A light through all the mists?

For, indeed, a light there is,
As I begin to see.
There is a God above all else
And He created me.

And so my praise returns to Him,
The made to please the Maker.
My every word is chosen now
For my own Chooser's pleasure.

And so the One who made the maker
Is Himself the reason.
The story for the story,
Designer of the season.

The inspiration for the painting,
Reason for the rhyme.
The Governor of nations
Until the end of time.

The Father of the architect,
The center of the movie –
If the makers will surrender
To the One who loves them truly.

Just think upon His wisdom,
Of all His majesty…
Think of how He gave you
This ability, and see:

If you don't desire to worship Him
On hearing all of this,
I pray that you will search
And soon discover what's amiss.

Confetti Sprinkles

Confetti sprinkles in my hair,
Confetti sprinkles everywhere!
Color doesn't matter much –
Sprinkles everywhere I touch!

Confetti sprinkles in the air,
Confetti falling from up there.
Confetti sprinkles in my mouth,
Happily headed straight down south.

Rainbow of confetti here,
Sprinkles falling, far and near.
Few notice that from up above,
Confetti pours down, full of love.

Open up your eyes and see:
The sprinkles land on you and me!
Confetti blessings fall for you;
May you see God loves you true.

When I turned 13, my youth group bought me a card and many of my friends signed it. I had never been celebrated like that and it made me feel so special! The card featured a cupcake and brightly colored sprinkles, and the phrase, "Pour on the blessings; sprinkle on the fun!" – and that was my inspiration to write this.

Life, Faith, Relationship

Happy New Year

Happy New Year, dear my friends!
I hope your year was sweet.
I pray you'll always find good times
And life will be a treat.

But life on earth is sorrow-filled
And I know it's true
That though you'll try to cheerful be,
You'll wind up sad and blue.

Two things remember then, I ask,
When it is, oh, so hard
To go on with your daily life,
When your joy is marred.

God is good and always there,
On Him you can depend.
And life is always easier
With good, believing friends.

Relationships with God and man
Will ease your path each day;
I love you all, and every day
For you I do pray.

I cannot wait to see you all,
And now I say to you:
May God bless and keep you
All through 2022!

Path of Life

I cannot wait to see you all,
Now as New Year arrives –
May God bless and keep you
All through 2025!

I cannot wait to see you all,
Now as the time befits –
May God bless and keep you
All through 2026!

I cannot wait to see you all
As I cry out to Heaven:
May God bless and keep you
All through 2027!

I cannot wait to see you all,
And since the hour's late –
May God bless and keep you
All through 2028!

I cannot wait to see you all,
And now I'll say my line:
May God bless and keep you
All through 2029!

I cannot wait to see you all,
Now as I say, you're worthy,
And may God bless and keep you
Through the year of 2030!

Life, Faith, Relationship

I cannot wait to see you all,
Now, just one word to come:
May God bless and keep you
All through 2031!

I cannot wait to see you all,
But till that time is here,
May God bless and keep you
All through 2033!

I cannot wait to see you all,
And now I'll say no more,
But may God bless and keep you
All through 2034!

I wrote this and sent it to my friend group at midnight, when the year 2022 began. I recently went through and added alternate endings for every possible year ending, just for fun.

About the Author

Tirzah Nilsson grew up reading older literature and passionately loving language and the way words can be used to communicate feelings. Finding the rhythm and beauty she always enjoyed sadly lacking in most modern work, she uses her own pen to bring those things to today's readers in a unique way. Her poetry collection *Path of Life: Reflections of a Soul in Bloom* brings to life the questions and struggles of her early years, offering glimpses of childlike faith, Biblical insight, and a wide-eyed appreciation of the natural world and its creatures. When she's not writing, her favorite pastimes range from crocheting to computer programming, always with her feline friend Misty by her side.

www.ingramcontent.com/pod-product-compliance
Lightning Source LLC
Chambersburg PA
CBHW060528080526
44586CB00012B/659